KidCaps' Presents

Jupiter:
Understanding Planets Just for Kids!

KidCaps is An Imprint of BookCaps™
www.bookcaps.com

Table of Contents

ABOUT KIDCAPS 4

WELCOME TO JUPITER 5

LESSON 1: ORIGINS, DISTANCE, SHAPE AND SIZE 8

1.1 HOW WAS JUPITER FORMED? 8
1.2 JUPITER: THE "FAILED" STAR 9
1.3 JUPITER FACTS: DISTANCE...9
1.4 JUPITER FACTS: SHAPE & SIZE...10
LESSON 1 REVIEW...12

LESSON 2: JUPITER'S ATMOSPHERE AND CORE 14

2.1 JUPITER THE GAS GIANT 14
2.2 THE GREAT RED SPOT 14
2.3 EXPLORING JUPITER'S ATMOSPHERE 17
2.4 DISCOVERING JUPITER'S CORE 21
LESSON 2 REVIEW...22

LESSON 3: JUPITER'S ORBIT 23

3.1 JUPITER AS A "COSMIC VACUUM CLEANER" 24
3.2 A YEAR ON JUPITER 25
3.3 A DAY ON JUPITER..26
LESSON 3 REVIEW...26

LESSON 4: JUPITER'S MOONS & RINGS.......................27

4.1 JUPITER'S MANY MOONS..28
4.2 DISCOVERING IO, EUROPA, GANYMEDE AND CALLISTO ..29
4.3 UNDERSTANDING TIDAL FLEXING 30
4.4 HANDS-ON LESSON: WHAT HEATS JUPITER'S MOONS?...32
4.5 MISSION TO JUPITER'S MOONS 33
4.6 JUPITER'S RINGS 34
LESSON 4 REVIEW...36

LESSON 5: MAGNETOSPHERE 38

5.1 WHAT IS A MAGNETOSPHERE?...38
5.2 JUPITER'S MAGNETOSPHERE: SIZE AND SHAPE 39

5.3 DISCOVERING JUPITER'S MAGNETOSPHERE....................41
5.4 IS JUPITER A PULSAR? 42
LESSON 5 REVIEW..43

LESSON 6: LIFE ON JUPITER? 44

6.1 LIFE ON JUPITER? 44
6.2 LIFE ON JUPITER'S MOONS?...45
6.3 DISCOVERING LIFE? 50
LESSON 6 REVIEW..50

LESSON REVIEW ANSWERS 51

LESSON 1 REVIEW..51
LESSON 2 REVIEW..52
LESSON 3 REVIEW..54
LESSON 4 EXPERIMENT QUESTIONS.......................................55
LESSON 4 REVIEW..56
LESSON 5 REVIEW..57
LESSON 6 REVIEW..59

About KidCaps

KidCaps is an imprint of BookCaps™ that is just for kids! Each month BookCaps will be releasing several books in this exciting imprint. Visit are website or like us on Facebook to see more!

Welcome to Jupiter

Welcome to the fifth planet from the sun! From our night sky, Jupiter looks like a bright star. Up close, however, Jupiter is massive gaseous ball with a giant red "eye" – a gas storm that has been raging for more than 300 years. The planet is made primarily of hydrogen, helium, methane and ammonium gases.

Jupiter is so big that more than 1,300 Earths could fit inside. As the largest planet in our solar system with 66 moons and a powerful magnetic and gravitational field, Jupiter forms its own miniature solar system. In fact, if Jupiter had been a little larger, the planet might have become its own star, like the sun.

A true-color composite image of Jupiter created from four different images captured by NASA's Cassini spacecraft. The dark spot in the image is shadow cast by Jupiter's moon, Europa.

Composite image created by Cassini spacecraft and NASA; public domain image not protected by copyright

This giant planet fascinated the Ancient Greeks and Romans. The Romans named the planet "Jupiter" after the Roman ruler of the gods. Today, Jupiter has been the focus of several NASA missions, including the Pioneer, Voyager, and Galileo missions. Currently, the spacecraft Juno is en route to Jupiter for further scientific exploration. Launched in 2011, Juno is expected to reach Jupiter in July 2016. The mission is name Juno after the Ancient Roman's name for Jupiter's wife.

Jupiter is the third largest object in the night sky, after Venus and the Moon. It can be seen at night with the naked eye ten months out of the year. With the aid of a basic telescope, Jupiter's gaseous cloud patterns and yellowish zones can be observed. With increased magnification, you can even see Jupiter's red eye.

Jupiter is a fascinating planet. Its moons may even hold the secrets to life in our Solar System outside of Earth. Ready to start exploring? Let's go!

Lesson 1: Origins, Distance, Shape and Size

1.1 How was Jupiter formed?

Jupiter, like the other gas planets, started out as tiny bits of ice. When our solar system was young, the outer regions were colder and more volatile than the inner regions. Ice and dust began to collide in the outer regions. Some ice particles stuck together during collision, building mass. As the ice particles became more massive, their gravity increased. This attracted even more dust, forming Jupiter's core. The massive core then attracted gases, creating Jupiter's atmosphere. Since Jupiter is very massive, it has a strong gravitational pull. This means that the heavier elements sink to the core, while the lighter elements, including helium and hydrogen, remain in the atmosphere.

1.2 Jupiter: The "Failed" Star

Jupiter is sometimes called the "failed" star. If Jupiter were slightly more massive, the pressure from the planet's mass would have caused the core temperature to reach the ignition point for thermonuclear fusion. Thermonuclear fusion is the process by which stars turn hydrogen into helium, releasing energy that causes the star to "shine". If Jupiter were 100 times more massive, we would have two stars in our solar system.

1.3 Jupiter Facts: Distance

Since both Jupiter and the Earth travel around the sun, the distance between these two planets varies. At their closest, Jupiter is 628,743,036 million kilometers from the Earth. At their farthest, the two planets are 928,081,020 million kilometers apart.

A second way to measure distance in outer space is by using astronomical units (AU). One AU is the mean distance between the Earth and the sun. That's the equivalent of 149,597,870.691 kilometers. This means the distance between the Earth and Jupiter ranges between 4.2 AU and 6.2 AU. Going from the Earth to Jupiter is the equivalent of traveling between the Earth and the sun at least four times.

The New Horizons space craft, launched in 2006 reached Jupiter in just 13 months. Other exploratory missions, however, have taken much longer. The Galileo spacecraft, launched in 1989, took six years to arrive. The Juno spacecraft, launched in 2011, is expected to arrive in 2016 If you were to travel to Jupiter at the speed of light, it would take between 32 and 42 minutes to reach the planet, depending on how far apart Earth and Jupiter are at the time. That's a lot faster than five years!

1.4 Jupiter Facts: Shape & Size

As the largest planet in our Solar System, Jupiter is very big. It would take more than 1,000 earths to fill up Jupiter. But even Jupiter looks small when compared with the sun! Here is a comparison to better understand how big (and small) Jupiter is when compared with the sun and Earth.

Top left: the sun, Jupiter and Earth; Top right: the sun and Jupiter; Bottom left: Earth and Jupiter; Bottom right: Earth and the Moon.

Because Jupiter is so big and dense, it has a very strong gravitational field and magnetic field. Because of the planet's immense gravity, it is sometimes called a "cosmic vacuum cleaner." This means that the planet sucks smaller, passing objects into orbit around it. We will discuss this more in Lesson 3.

A strong gravitational field also means that you would weigh two and half times as much on Jupiter as you would weigh on Earth. If you traveled to Jupiter on vacation, you would be very heavy! For example, if you weigh 80 pounds here on Earth and traveled to Jupiter, you would be exactly the same size, but feel as if you weighed 200 pounds.

Because Jupiter spins so fast, the middle of the planet is stretched out. Imagine someone spinning pizza dough very fast to make it stretch. That's similar to what has happened to Jupiter. Rather than being a perfect sphere like Earth, Jupiter is short and fat. Jupiter's shape is called an *oblate spheroid.*

Lesson 1 Review

1. How was Jupiter formed?
2. Could Jupiter have become a star?
3. How much would you weigh on Jupiter?
4. What is an Astronomical Unit?
5. Why does Jupiter have a unique shape?

Lesson 2: Jupiter's Atmosphere and Core

2.1 Jupiter the Gas Giant

Jupiter is the first of the "gas giant" planets located outside the asteroid belt. The other gas giants are Saturn, Uranus and Neptune. The planets are called "gas giants" because they are made up entirely of dense layers of gas. They are sometimes referred to as the "Jovian" planets.

As a gas planet, Jupiter does not have a solid surface. The lowest level of Jupiter's atmosphere transitions directly into Jupiter's fluid interior. In fact, it's impossible to "walk" on Jupiter the way we walk on earth. There is no distinction between the atmosphere and the surface; one seamlessly blends into the other forming an ocean of liquid gas.

2.2 The Great Red Spot

One of Jupiter's most distinctive features is its red eye. Formally named the "Great Red Spot", this gas storm is actually twice the size of Earth. The storm has raged for more than 300 years.

The Great Red Spot, as captured by Voyager 1 in 1979.
Image created by Voyager 1 spacecraft and NASA; public domain image not protected by copyright

Scientist Robert Hooke first observed the Great Red Spot in 1664. Over the last several hundred years, the Great Red Spot has been observed to fade from vision on several occasions, as well as change locations on the planet's surface. Astronomers do not know why the Great Red Spot is red. Theories suggest that the red color may be caused by red phosphorus or another sulfur compound.

The Great Red Spot is classified as an "anticyclonic storm". This means that the Great Red Spot is a high pressure storm with wind flowing from areas of high pressure to low pressure. The Great Red Spot rotates counterclockwise and moves independent of Jupiter's atmosphere. Unlike the anticyclonic storms on Earth that are powered by water, the Great Red Spot is powered by smaller storms merging together. Warmer gases rise into a column of cold air, creating a vortex that powers the storm. Other famous extraterrestrial anticyclonic storms include Anne's Spot on Saturn and the Great Dark Spot on Neptune.

Jupiter's second most distinctive feature is the "Oval BA" storm, which is also known by the names "Red Spot, Jr.", "The Little Red Spot" and "Red, Jr." Oval BA is located in Jupiter's Southern hemisphere near the Great Red Spot. It is similar in appearance to the Great Red Spot, although the storm is much smaller. Oval BA was first identified in 2000 when several smaller white storms appeared to merge together. In 2006, astronomers observed the storm turning red. According to observations from the Hubble Telescope, Oval BA is gathering strength. As of July 2008, Oval BA was approximately the same size as Earth (making it half the size of the Great Red Spot) with winds moving at speeds up to 618 kilometers per hour.

Oval BA and the Great Red Spot are located on separate hemispheric bands that move independent of each other. For this reason, the two storms occasionally travel close to one another. However, the storms have not yet merged.

2.3 Exploring Jupiter's Atmosphere

Imagine that you are on a trip to visit Jupiter. As you first enter Jupiter's atmosphere from outer space, it is cold and thin. As you descend further, the atmosphere becomes thicker and warmer, eventually turning into a hot, dark fog of poisonous gas. In this darkness, the pressure becomes so intense that the gases in the atmosphere turn into an ocean of liquid gas.

Here on Earth, there is a separation between our liquid covering (the ocean) and our atmosphere. On a nice day, you might go to the beach and float on the ocean. On Jupiter, however, this is not possible. There is no distinction between the liquid and the gas; they seamlessly merge into one.

Jupiter's atmosphere is made primarily of molecular hydrogen (H_2) and helium. The atmosphere also contains methane, hydrogen sulfide, ammonia, phosphine and water. These simple compounds tell scientists that the planet is rich in carbon, nitrogen, sulfur and oxygen. There are also trace amounts of other gases and compounds. Colliding comets, such as Shoemaker-Levy 9, may cause the presence of carbon dioxide, carbon monoxide and oxygen in the upper atmosphere. Scientists estimate Jupiter's atmospheric composition based on information gathered from the Galileo and Cassini spacecraft, the Infrared Space Observatory (ISO) and observations made here on Earth.

What causes Jupiter's weather patterns?
On Earth, the energy to power our weather cycle is generated from sunlight. Since Jupiter is so far from the sun, the planet receives very little energy from sunlight. The energy that powers Jupiter's turbulent weather is generated from the planet's dense core.

Here on Earth, the jet stream moves clouds across our sky, bringing rain, snow or other changes to our weather. On Jupiter, the jet stream moves really fast! Clouds of gas fly by at speeds up to 400 miles per hour. Gases that move up towards the top of Jupiter's atmosphere bring clouds of ammonia from the lower layers.

What causes Jupiter's gas storms?

On Jupiter, the atmosphere is so dense and cold that it behaves like a fluid, rather than a gas. Fluid mechanics predicts how Jupiter's gases will move. One pattern of movement creates wave-like features where different densities of gas meet. A second pattern of movement creates a steady stream of one type of gas. A steady stream of movement can sometimes break into individual eddies. These eddies can form Jupiter's storms, known as cyclones.

What do the different colored bands in Jupiter's atmosphere mean?

When you look at a photo of Jupiter, you can see that the planet is divided into distinct and colorful bands of gas. The different colors represent different depths of Jupiter's atmosphere. Jupiter has two types of bands: dark colored belts and light colored zones.

Annotated image of Jupiter showing the different belts and zones; image originally captured by the Cassini spacecraft.
Licensed under Creative Commons Attribution-Share Alike 3.0 Unported license; picture of Jupiter taken by Cassini spacecraft, annotated and modified by Awolf002.

The dark clouds in Jupiter's belts are thin and located at low altitudes. These clouds are different shades of red, brown, orange and yellow. Astronomers believe that these colors are caused by chemical reactions with sulfur, phosphorous and carbon in Jupiter's atmosphere.

The light colored zones have dense clouds of ammonia ice located at high altitudes. The white and blue colors in these clouds are caused by frozen carbon dioxide and ice. Brown ovals are low-pressure systems in the northern hemisphere. White ovals are high-pressure systems in the southern hemisphere.

Jets mark the transition between bands and zones. Eastward moving jets are winds that move away from Jupiter's equator, transitioning from zones to belts. Westward moving jets are winds the move towards the equator, transitioning from zones to bands.

2.4 Discovering Jupiter's Core

At the center of Jupiter is a dense, rocky core. This core is only slightly larger than the Earth, but it weighs 20 times more than our planet weighs. Jupiter's dense core means that the planet's magnetic field is also very strong.

How do we know that Jupiter has a small core?

While we have never visited Jupiter in person, we can extrapolate that the planet has a very small core in relation to its size. As a planet, Jupiter is oblate rather than spherical. We also know that Jupiter has a high rotation rate. A high rotation rate, in combination with a small core, is what creates an oblate shape. Based on the laws of physics, we know that the smaller the core, the more oblate the shape. Consequently, scientists have extrapolated that since Jupiter is very oblate, the planet must have a very small core relative to its very large size.

Lesson 2 Review

1. What is a "gas giant"?
2. What is the Great Red Spot?
3. What is inside Jupiter's atmosphere?
4. Does Jupiter have a surface?
5. What causes Jupiter's different colors?
6. How do we know that Jupiter has a small core?

Lesson 3: Jupiter's Orbit

Jupiter is the first planet in our Solar System located outside the asteroid belt. It is the fifth planet from the sun.

The sun and eight planets in our Solar System shown by relative size and distance to one another.
Licensed under Creative Commons Attribution-Share Alike 3.0 Unported license; originally created by Dave Jarvis

Unlike Earth, Jupiter's axis is at a very slight tilt. This means that the planet does not experience the same seasonal changes that we experience here on Earth.

Because Jupiter's orbit is beyond Earth's orbit, the planet always appears to be fully illuminated when viewed through telescopes here on Earth. It is only during spacecraft missions to Jupiter that we can observe a crescent view of the planet.

3.1 Jupiter as a "Cosmic Vacuum Cleaner"

Scientists believe that Jupiter's large size and position just outside the asteroid belt played a role in the development of life on Earth. Because Jupiter is so massive, it sucks anything that passes by into its gravitational field. Scientists witnessed the power of Jupiter first-hand in 1994, when the comet Shoemaker Levy 9 collided with Jupiter. The planet's powerful gravitational field ripped the comet apart into 21 pieces prior to impact. If Shoemaker Levy 9 had hit Earth, the results would have been devastating. For this reason, scientists believe that Jupiter's unique position in our Solar System has helped prevent numerous asteroid and comet collisions.

Scientists widely believe that an asteroid caused the extinction of the dinosaurs. Without Jupiter to "vacuum up" passing asteroids and comets, scientists hypothesize that many more cataclysmic extinctions might have occurred on Earth. Frequent extinction events could have made the development of complex life difficult. While the full impact of Jupiter's presence as a cosmic vacuum cleaner is not completely known, scientists do believe that the planet's position and size may have positively impacted the development of life on Earth.

3.2 A Year on Jupiter

The planets in our Solar System all take different amounts of time to complete a single orbit around the sun. Here on Earth, it takes 365 days to complete one orbit, so one year on Earth is 365 days. Since Jupiter is much further from the sun, it takes 11.9 Earth years to complete one orbit. That means one year on Jupiter is nearly 12 times as long as one year on Earth!

3.3 A Day on Jupiter

While a year on Jupiter is very long, a day on the planet is very short. Here on Earth, it takes 24 hours, the equivalent of one full day, for the Earth to complete a full rotation on its axis. Jupiter, however, spins very quickly on its axis. Jupiter completes a full spin every 9.84 hours – that's a very short day!

Because Jupiter is a gas giant and not a solid body, the planet does not rotate evenly. The rotation of Jupiter's polar atmosphere is about five minutes slower that Jupiter's equatorial rotation. This means if you were visiting Jupiter's north pole, a day on Jupiter would last five minutes longer than if you were visiting the planet's equator.

Lesson 3 Review

1. Why is Jupiter called a "cosmic vacuum cleaner"?
2. How long is a year on Jupiter?
3. How long is a day on Jupiter?
4. Does Jupiter have seasons like we do on Earth?

Lesson 4: Jupiter's Moons & Rings

Jupiter has at least 66 moons. Using a basic telescope or a pair of binoculars, scientists and at-home sky watchers can spot Jupiter's four largest moons. These four are named Io, Europa, Ganymede and Callisto. The four largest moons are called the Galilean moons because the famous Italian astronomer Galileo Galilei who discovered them in 1610. Galileo used an early telescope to identify the four moons. His discovery was the first time that anyone had identified objects orbiting another planet. Galileo's discovery paved the way for scientists to understand that the Earth rotates around the sun, rather than our Solar System rotating around the Earth.

4.1 Jupiter's Many Moons

In addition to the four Galilean moons, astronomers have formally named 46 other moons that orbit Jupiter. These moons are small and likely former asteroids that became trapped in Jupiter's orbit. These named moons include the four closest to Jupiter, known as the "inner moons." Many of these moons are named for different female characters in Roman mythology that had relationships with the Roman god Jupiter. NASA scientists identify the other moons as "provisional moons." These are smaller satellites that are given a series of numbers and letters for their name.

Many of Jupiter's moons were once asteroids traveling through the solar system. Since Jupiter is a very large gaseous planet, asteroids that passed close to the planet easily fell into orbit. This is why Jupiter has so many moons in comparison to other planets.

Close to the planet, Jupiter's moons travel at very high speeds. In fact, some of these moons circle Jupiter multiple times in a single Earth day. Because of Jupiter's powerful magnetic field, the planet has captured passing asteroids as far as 20,000 miles beyond the planet. These far-out moons may take more than two Earth years to make a single trip around Jupiter.

4.2 Discovering Io, Europa, Ganymede and Callisto

Io, Europa, Ganymede and Callisto are Jupiter's four most famous moons.

Jupiter's four moons, Io, Europa, Ganymede and Callisto.
Composite image created by Galileo spacecraft and NASA; public domain image not protected by copyright

Each of these four moons has unique features:
- Io is the most volcanically active object in our Solar System, with more volcanic activity than any other planet or moon. Io is also very close in size to Earth's moon.
- Europa's surface is made primarily of ice water. NASA researchers believe that Europa may have twice as much water as Earth. For this reason, scientists believe that of all the planets and moons in our Solar System, the greatest chance for discovering life is on Europa.

- Ganymede is the largest moon in the solar system, bigger than even the planet Mercury. It is also the only moon in the solar system to have its own magnetic field.
- Callisto's surface is heavily marked with craters. Scientists believe these craters are extremely ancient, and may even date from the very beginning of our Solar System.

Io, Europa and Ganymede have an interesting relationship with each other. The three moons orbit Jupiter in a similar manner. Every time Ganymede completes one orbit, Europa completes two orbits and Io completes four orbits. The moons always keep the same "face" towards Jupiter. This means each moon makes a complete orbit on its axis in the same amount of time that it takes the moon to orbit around Jupiter.

Io, located between Ganymede and Europa, is also trapped in a tug of war between these two moons.

4.3 Understanding Tidal Flexing

Jupiter's inner moons, Io and Europa, are very different from our Moon. Instead of being cold, barren landscapes, Io and Europa have warm cores. In fact, Io has the most volcanic activity of any planet or moon in our Solar System. This is due to *tidal flexing*.

What is tidal flexing?

Here on Earth, the ocean's high tide and low tide are caused by the moon's gravitational pull on the Earth. The moon pulls on all parts of the Earth, although this pull is strongest on the side of the Earth that is closest to the moon. While the difference is only a small fraction of a percent, this difference is enough to distort the Earth's shape and cause a high tide or low tide. Scientists define a "tide" as a "distortion in the shape of one body induced by the gravitational pull of another nearby object." While our understanding of tides here on Earth is based on the movement of the ocean, a tide can also refer to the movement of solid rock. That's what happens with Jupiter's moons.

How does Jupiter's gravity affect Io?
Io travels around Jupiter in an elliptical orbit. This means that sometimes Io is closer to Jupiter, while other times it is closer to Jupiter's other moons. When Io is close to Jupiter, Jupiter's gravity stretches Io into the shape of an egg. When Io is away from Jupiter, the moon relaxes into a spherical shape. However, as Io moves further from Jupiter, Ganymede and Europa also pull on Io. This means that Io is trapped in a constant tug-of-war between powerful Jupiter, Ganymede and Europa.

When Jupiter's gravity force flexes Io, its surface will rise and fall, just like the Earth's surfaces moves in response to the Moon's gravity. However, since the difference in size between Jupiter and Io is much greater than the difference between the Earth and the Moon, the effects of tidal flexing on Io are also much greater than the Moon's pull on the Earth. The flexing of solid rock inside Io causes the moon's core to heat up. Solid rock melts into magma, causing volcanic eruptions. This is why Io is the moon with the most volcanic activity in our solar system.

4.4 Hands-on Lesson: What Heats Jupiter's Moons?

This hands-on lesson will help you understand tidal flexing and explain why Io and Europa have warm cores.

What you need:
- 2 hand-sized rubber balls
- 2 small thermometers

What to do:
1. Cut a small, single hole inside each foam ball that is just large enough to insert a thermometer.
2. Record the interior temperature of both balls.
3. Hold one ball in your left hand but do not squeeze it.

4. Hold the second ball in your right hand and squeeze it for five minutes.
5. Record the interior temperature of both balls after five minutes.

Questions to answer:
1. What happened on the temperature of the ball that was not squeezed?
2. How quickly did the temperature of the squeezed ball increase? (Divide the temperature difference by five minutes to find the rate of temperature increase per minute)
3. What is the maximum temperature of the control ball? What is the maximum temperature of the flexed ball?

4.5 Mission to Jupiter's Moons

Because of the possibility of life on Europa, NASA scientists would like to study Jupiter's moons in greater detail. Unfortunately, funding challenges led to the cancellation of NASA's JIMO (Jupiter Icy Moons Orbiter) mission. A new mission led by the European Space Agency ESA) named Jupiter Icy Moons Explorer (JUICE) is currently set to explore Ganymede, Callisto, and Europa. A major goal for the JUICE mission is to explore whether liquid water exists beneath Europa's icy surface. JUICE is scheduled to launch in 2022, reaching the moons in 2030. If the mission goes as planned, JUICE will be the first robotic spacecraft to explore an ocean on another world.

4.6 Jupiter's Rings

Jupiter has four rings. They are faint and only visible when the planet passes directly in front of the sun. When Jupiter passes directly in front of the sun, light illuminates the rings and makes them visible here on Earth. Even then, the rings are extremely difficult to observe. The thick inner ring is called the 'halo', the thin middle ring is called the 'main ring', and the two thick outer rings are called the 'gossamer rings'. Unlike Saturn's rings, which are made from ice, Jupiter's rings are made from dust. This dust is likely from collisional debris and material ejected by Jupiter's different moons. This is also why it is difficult to see Jupiter's rings. Saturn's ice rings reflect a large amount of the sun's light. Jupiter's dust rings reflect very little light.

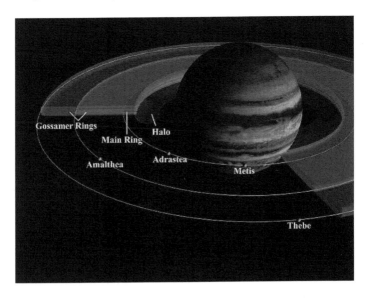

Jupiter's four rings, along with the location of the planet's moons named Adrastea, Metis, Thebe and Amalthea.
Image created by NASA; public domain image not protected by copyright

Dust particles do not last long in Jupiter's rings. Jupiter's powerful magnetosphere pulls the dust particles out of rotation and closer to the planet. If any ice particles enter the rings, this ice quickly evaporates. Consequently, astronomers believe the collisions between Jupiter's outer moons and asteroids constantly create new dust to replace particles that are pulled away by Jupiter's magnetosphere. For example, scientists believe that collisions with two of Jupiter's moons, Amalthea and Thebe, created the outer gossamer rings.

Since Jupiter's rings are difficult to see, astronomers only recently discovered their existence. In 1975, information from the Pioneer 11 spacecraft first led astronomers to guess that the rings existed. Their existence was not officially confirmed until four years later. In 1979, the Voyager 1 spacecraft captured the very first image of Jupiter's rings. The Galileo orbiter, New Horizons spacecraft and Cassini spacecraft have all helped astronomers learn new information about the rings.

Lesson 4 Review

1. How many moons does Jupiter have?
2. What are the names of the four major moons? List one unique characteristic of each moon.
3. What is tidal flexing?
4. Describe Jupiter's rings. How are they different from Saturn's rings?

Lesson 5: Magnetosphere

5.1 What is a Magnetosphere?

A magnetosphere is a scientific term for the magnetic field created by a planetary body. The magnetosphere is the region of magnetic influence exerted by the Earth or another planet, like Jupiter. When charged particles, such as ions, enter Jupiter's magnetosphere, their movement is influenced by Jupiter's magnetic field.

Earth's magnetosphere is essential to our daily existence. The magnetosphere protects our fragile ozone layer from the solar wind. The solar wind is a stream of ionized particles emitted by the sun. Without protection, these powerful particles could damage Earth's atmosphere and destroy the ozone layer. The ozone layer protects life on Earth from ultraviolet radiation. Without Earth's ozone layer and magnetosphere, life as we know it would cease to exist. For example, the planet Mars has virtually no magnetosphere to protect it. Consequently, scientists believe that one reason there is no life on Mars is because the planet lost its water due to the harsh solar wind. If Mars had a magnetosphere, larger quantities of water might exist, making life as we know possible.

5.2 Jupiter's Magnetosphere: Size and Shape

Jupiter's magnetic field is 19,000 times stronger than Earth's magnetic field. Think of it as a radiation hot zone of staggering intensity. Incoming charged particles from the sun are whipped into a frenzy. If you were traveling to Jupiter with your smartphone and iPod, they'd both be fried – as would most of your electronics, thanks to the field's intensity.

Jupiter's magnetosphere is the largest thing in our solar system. If it were visible from Earth, it would be the same size as our full moon in the sky – even though Jupiter is millions of kilometers further away.

The electrical currents that flow through Jupiter's core create the planet's magnetosphere. The magnetosphere is also influenced by the volcanic eruptions on Jupiter's moon, Io. These eruptions eject large quantities of sulfur dioxide into the atmosphere. Because Io's atmosphere is extremely thin, these eruptions also impact Jupiter's magnetosphere.

The sun also affects the shape of a Jupiter's magnetosphere. Jupiter's magnetosphere blocks the solar wind from entering, diverting it away from the planet. The diagram below shows how the solar wind shapes Jupiter's magnetosphere.

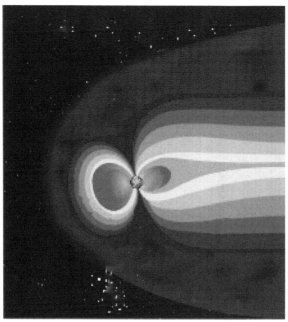

Jupiter's magnetosphere, including the long tail stretching out towards Saturn's orbit.
Edited version of a public domain image originally created by NASA

While the magnetosphere is spherical on the side of the planet facing the sun, it is long and thin, like a tail, on the side facing away from the sun. This is because the solar wind stretches out the back of Jupiter's magnetosphere, creating what astronomer's call a "magnetotail". At times, the solar wind can extend Jupiter's "magnetotail" as far as Saturn's orbit.

5.3 Discovering Jupiter's Magnetosphere

Jupiter's core is primarily made of metallic hydrogen. This metallic shell generates an intense magnetic field that also emits radio waves. Radio waves are a type of electromagnetic radiation. Here on Earth, our radios pick up waves that are set to specific frequencies for broadcasting music. The radio waves produced by Jupiter's magnetosphere have a very low frequency that cannot be detected by our radios. However, in the early days of radio transmission, some broadband radio receivers were set to pick up a much wider spectrum of waves. This is how scientists may have first discovered Jupiter's magnetic field.

In 1899, the scientist Nikola Tesla was using an early broadband radio receiver to listen to radio waves from outer space. Tesla picked up Jupiter's shortwave radio emissions, but he could not clearly identify their origin. At the time when Tesla made his observations, Jupiter and Mars were located very close in the night sky. Consequently, Tesla confused the radio wave origin, believing that he was listening to sounds being emitted from Mars. It was not until 1955 that scientists conclusively identified Jupiter's magnetic field when they discovered decametric radio emissions coming from the planet. This discovery helped astronomers estimate the strength of Jupiter's magnetosphere.

NASA's Pioneer missions in the 1970s made an initial exploration of Jupiter's magnetosphere, testing the field's power and strength. Scientists had long wondered how the planet generated giant magnetic storms inside a ball of gas. They also wondered why one of Jupiter's moons boiling over with volcanic activity – while the other moon was covered in ice. These fly-by missions paved the way for future Jupiter exploration, including discoveries regarding Jupiter's metallic hydrogen core, the cause for the planet's storms and Io's volcanic activity.

5.4 Is Jupiter a Pulsar?

A pulsar is a highly magnetized star. Like a deep space lighthouse, a pulsar star emits a stream of electromagnetic radiation. Because pulsar stars rotate, the star's beam of electromagnetic radiation can only be observed when it is pointing straight at the observer. This is similar to the light emitted from a lighthouse; since a lighthouse's beam rotates, it is best seen when it is pointed directly at a ship. Because pulsar stars produce a regular beam of electromagnetic radiation, astronomers sometimes call them "atomic clocks" for their accurate timing.

Like pulsar stars, Jupiter's rotation affects the planet's radio and particle emissions. The planet also emits electromagnetic radiation at steady intervals, just like a pulsar star. However, Jupiter is a planet, not a star. Consequently astronomers say that Jupiter has some "pulsar-like" characteristics, but it is not a pulsar star.

Lesson 5 Review

1. What is a magnetosphere?
2. Why is Earth's magnetosphere important?
3. Describe Jupiter's magnetosphere.
4. How was Jupiter's magnetosphere discovered?
5. In what ways is Jupiter like a Pulsar star?

Lesson 6: Life on Jupiter?

Is life on Jupiter possible? At first glance, the gaseous planet looks like the last place anyone would want to live! The planet's moons, however, may hold the secret to life outside our Earth.

6.1 Life on Jupiter?

In 1956, scientists Stanley Miller and Harold Urey conducted an experiment that showed simple organic compounds, including the building blocks of proteins and macromolecules, could be created from the combination of different gases and energy. In the experiment, Miller and Urey combined water, methane, ammonia, and hydrogen. They used an electrical current to simulate lightening. The combination of the gases, along with the electrical energy, resulted in the formation of amino acids, sugars and lipids. This experiment showed how organic life may have been created on Earth. Could the same process occur on Jupiter?

Jupiter's atmosphere is rich in methane, ammonia and hydrogen, three chemicals used to generate life in Miller and Urey's experiment. However, there is little water in Jupiter's atmosphere. The high temperatures within the atmosphere's interior also break down methane and ammonia. Scientists have concludes that the likelihood for basic life forms, or even the building blocks of life, are virtually impossible on Jupiter

6.2 Life on Jupiter's Moons?

Is it possible for life to exist on Jupiter's moons? For many years, scientists have theorized that basic life forms could exist on Europa. NASA lists Europa towards the top of the short list of places in our solar system that might harbor extraterrestrial life.

Europa, as viewed by the Galileo spacecraft.
Image created by Galileo spacecraft and NASA;
public domain image not protected by copyright

Why is life possible on Europa? Scientists theorize that Europa's icy crust could be covering a sea of liquid water. This water might be able to sustain organisms. Scientists also theorize that similar conditions could exist on Ganymede and Callisto. All three moons may also have sources of energy that could help support life. An internal source of energy is important since the moons are so far from the sun and receive little sunlight. Previous studies have hinted that all three moons could harbor liquid oceans—and maybe life forms—below their icy surfaces. However, scientists believe Europa is the best possibility for life. Friction from tidal stretching could heat Europa's core enough to create a liquid ocean underneath the moon's icy covering.

Scientists believe that a process called "repaving" could explain how oxygen is circulated through Europa's icy ocean. Friction from tidal stretching would cause warmer ocean material to ooze up towards the frozen surface. At the same time, older ice would sink and melt towards the interior. The cycle of "repaving" also explains why the ice currently covering Europa looks "young". The ice covering lacks the characteristic markings of frequent meteor collisions that typically cover moons. When charged particles from Jupiter's magnetic field hit Europa, oxygen is created. This oxygen is then circulated through the ocean through the repaving process. Scientists estimate that it might have taken one to two billion years for the very first oxygen to reach the bottom of the ocean. According to scientists, oxygen must be introduced slowly into an environment in order for organisms to learn to tolerate oxygen's presence and become dependent on it. If the repaving process on Europa move slowly and steadily, then it is possible that oxygen was introduced slowly and consistently, which is essential to supporting life.

Clues to how life might exist on Europa lie deep within the Arctic Circle. Europa's extensive sub-surface ocean may be heated by volcanic vents - much like the vents that are found along fault lines under Earth's oceans. Where there is water, simple microorganisms may thrive. New research suggests that Europa could have enough oxygen to support life. This is important because where there is a highly oxygenated sub-surface ocean, more complex creatures may have evolved. Any life that does exist would be protected from dangerous space radiation by the icy crust.

Not all scientists believe that life may exist on Europa. This is because Europa is trapped in a planetary tug-of-war with Jupiter and Io. It is possible that Io could be pushing or pulling on Europa in extreme cycles, affecting the rate of surface repaving. If the surface repaving does not happen at a consistent rate, then this could affect the rate at which oxygen reaches into Europa's ocean. Inconsistent tidal activity could also change the rate at which heat and nutrients are available. This is one reason why some scientists think that the possibility for any life forms beyond a basic microbe is very slim.

So, could microbes, multicellular organisms, maybe even a terrestrial jellyfish, exist on Europa? Maybe; however, until we land a research mission on Europa, we may never know for sure.

6.3 Discovering Life?

In May 2012, the European Space Agency (ESA) announced the Jupiter Icy Moon Explorer (JUICE) mission. JUICE will study Jupiter's atmosphere, as well as Europa, Ganymede and Callisto. The mission will scan the moons' surfaces for subsurface water reservoirs and study the physical properties of the moons' icy crusts. The mission is not expected to launch until 2022, however, and it won't reach Jupiter until 2030. We may have to wait a long time for answers!

Lesson 6 Review

1. Is life possible on Jupiter? Why or why not?
2. Is life possible on Europa? Why or why not?

Lesson Review Answers

Lesson 1 Review

1. *How was Jupiter formed?*
   Jupiter, like the other Jovian planets, was formed when bits of ice and dust collided and created larger chunks. As these chunks became increasingly massive, they created a strong, dense core. This density attracted gas, creating Jupiter's atmosphere.

2. *Could Jupiter have become a star?*
   Yes – if the planet were 100 times more massive, the planet's core temperature would have reached the ignition point for thermonuclear fusion Our solar system would then have two stars intend of just one.

3. How much would you weigh on Jupiter?
   Jupiter's strong gravitational field means that you would weigh 2.5 times more on Jupiter than you do here on Earth. If you weigh 80 pounds on Earth, you will weigh 200 pounds on Jupiter.

4. *Why does Jupiter have a unique shape?*
   Jupiter's shape is called an oblate spheroid; it

is short and fat. This is because Jupiter's core is very dense and the planet spins very fast. This combination of a dense core and fast rotation causes the planet to be stretched out, rather than a perfect sphere.

Lesson 2 Review

1. *What is a "gas giant"?*
   A gas giant is the name for the planets in our Solar System that are located outside the asteroid belt. Jupiter is the first of the gas giants. The other gas giants are Saturn, Uranus and Neptune. These planets are sometimes called the "Jovian" planets after Roman mythology.

2. *What is the Great Red Spot?*
   The Great Red Spot is a swirling gas storm that is twice the size of Earth. Sometimes called Jupiter's "Red Eye", the Great Red Spot is one of the planet's most distinctive features. The storm has raged for more than 300 years.

3. *Describe Jupiter's atmosphere.*
   Jupiter's atmosphere consists primarily of molecular hydrogen (H_2) and helium. The atmosphere also contains methane, hydrogen sulfide, ammonia, phosphine and water. The outside of the planet's atmosphere is thin and

cold. Closer in to the core, the atmosphere is hot, dark fog of poisonous gas.

4. *Does Jupiter have a surface?*
No. The pressure on Jupiter is so intense that the gases in the planet's atmosphere merge into an ocean of liquid gas. Because of the planet's high pressure, there is no surface to this ocean.

5. *What do Jupiter's different colors mean?*
When you look at a photo of Jupiter, you can see that the planet is divided into distinct and colorful bands of gas. The red, brown, orange and yellow colors are caused by chemical reactions to sulfur. The white and blue colors are caused by frozen carbon dioxide and ice. Brown ovals are low-pressure systems in the northern hemisphere. White ovals are high-pressure systems in the southern hemisphere.

6. *How do we know that Jupiter has a small core?*
While scientists have never measured Jupiter's core, they believe that the core is very small in relation to Jupiter's big size. Unlike Earth, Jupiter is an oblate shape, which means the planet is flattened in the middle. Based on the laws of physics, a planet can only have an oblate shape if it has a very small core and also spins very fast. Scientists already know that Jupiter spins very fast for its very large size. Consequently, scientists

believe that Jupiter's core is very small in comparison to the planet's very large size.

Lesson 3 Review

1. *Why is Jupiter called a "cosmic vacuum cleaner"?*
   Because of Jupiter's large size and position just outside the asteroid belt, the Jupiter attracts many passing asteroids and comets into its gravitational field. The planet appears to "vacuum up" passing objects. Some scientists believe that Jupiter may have positively influenced the development of life on Earth. By "vacuuming up" passing asteroids, Jupiter may have limited the number of cataclysmic extinctions that occurred on Earth, allowing for the development of complex life.

2. *How long is a year on Jupiter?*
   A year on Jupiter is very long – it takes the planet 11.9 Earth years to complete one orbit around the sun.

3. *How long is a day on Jupiter?*
   A day on Jupiter is very short. The planet completes a full spin every 9.84 Earth hours. That means Jupiter experiences nearly three days in the time it takes for Earth to experience one.

4. *Does Jupiter have seasons like we do on Earth?*
Jupiter's axis is at a very slight tilt. This means that the planet does not have seasons like we do on Earth.

Lesson 4 Experiment Questions

1. *What happened on the temperature of the ball that was not squeezed?*
The temperature of the control ball should never be warmer than 98.6 degrees, the body temperature of the person who is holding the ball.

2. *How quickly did the temperature of the squeezed ball increase?*
Divide the temperature difference by five minutes to find the rate of temperature increase per minute.

3. *What is the maximum temperature of the control ball? What is the maximum temperature of the flexed ball?*
The control ball can never exceed 98.6 degrees. In theory, the ball that is being squeezed could eventually melt and flow out of your hand. You would need to squeeze it a VERY long time for this to happen, however! The action of you squeezing the ball reflects

the same "squeeze" that Io receives from tidal flexing. This is why Io is home to so much volcanic activity.

Lesson 4 Review

1. *How many moons does Jupiter have?*
Jupiter has at least 66 moons. Astronomers have formally named 50 moons that orbit Jupiter. Astronomers have labeled the remaining moons as "provisional moons", using a series of numbers and letters to identify them.

2. *What are the names of the four major moons? List one unique characteristic of each moon.*
Italian astronomer Galileo Galilei discovered Jupiter's four most famous moons. They are named Io, Europa, Ganymede and Callisto. Io has the most volcanic activity of any moon or planet in our Solar System. Europa is covered in ice. Scientists believe that the greatest chance for discovering life is on Europa. Ganymede is the largest moon in the solar system, bigger than even the planet Mercury. Callisto's surface is heavily marked with craters dating from the early days of the Solar System.

3. *What is tidal flexing?*
Tidal flexing is the gravitational effect that

one object has on another. When Jupiter's gravity force flexes Io, the moon's surface will rise and fall. The flexing of solid rock inside Io causes the its core to heat up. Solid rock melts into magma, causing volcanic eruptions. This is why Io is the moon with the most volcanic activity in our solar system.

4. *Describe Jupiter's rings. How are they different from Saturn's rings?*
Jupiter has four rings made from dust that are only visible when the planet passes directly in front of the sun. Saturn's rings are more numerous and easily visible because they are made from ice, which reflects light better than dust.

Lesson 5 Review

1. *What is a magnetosphere?*
A magnetosphere is a scientific term for the magnetic field created by a planetary body. The magnetosphere is the region of magnetic influence exerted by the Earth or another planet, like Jupiter.

2. *Why is Earth's magnetosphere important?*
Earth's magnetosphere protects our fragile ozone layer from the solar wind. Without protection, the solar wind could destroy the ozone layer, exposing life to dangerous

ultraviolet radiation. If this happens, life as we know it could cease to exist.

3. *Describe Jupiter's magnetosphere.*
Jupiter's magnetosphere is the largest thing in our solar system. If it were visible from Earth, it would be the same size as our full moon in the sky. The magnetosphere is spherical in the front of the planet with a long tail in the back, called a "magnetotail". Sometimes the magnetotail extends as far back as Saturn's orbit.

4. *How was Jupiter's magnetosphere discovered?*
Scientists believe that Nicola Tesla first detected low frequency radio waves emitted from Jupiter's magnetosphere. However, Tesla mistakenly thought these radio waves were coming from Mars. It was not until fifty years later that scientists discovered radio emissions coming from the planet. Exploration mission, such as the Pioneer mission in the 1970s, allowed NASA researchers to test the magnetosphere's size and strength.

5. *In what ways is Jupiter like a Pulsar star?*
A pulsar star emits a steady stream of electromagnetic radiation. As the star rotates, the electromagnetic radiation appears to "pulsate", just like the flashing beams of light emitted from a lighthouse. Like a pulsar star,

Jupiter's rotation affects the planet's radio and particle emissions. However, Jupiter is classified as a planet, rather than a star.

Lesson 6 Review

1. *Is life possible on Jupiter? Why or why not?* Scientists do not believe that life is possible on Jupiter. While Jupiter's atmosphere is rich in methane, ammonia and hydrogen, three chemicals necessary to generate life, the atmosphere has very little water. additionally, the high temperatures on Jupiter likely cause methane and ammonia to break down. Consequently, scientists have concluded that the even amino acids, the basic building blocks of life, could not exist on Jupiter.

2. *Is life possible on Europa? Why or why not?* Scientists believe that very basic terrestrial life forms could exist on Europa. Scientists theorize that underneath Europa's icy crust is a sea of liquid water. Europa also has its own internal source of energy, a heated core, which is essential to supporting life this far from the sun. The moon's subsurface ocean could be heated by volcanic vents, which would create an environment where simple microorganism could thrive. Research also suggests that Europa has enough oxygen to support basic life in its oceans. Tidal flexing could cause the

oceans to be repaved slowly over millions of years, circulating nutrients, heat and oxygen through the waters that would be necessary for life.

Made in the USA
San Bernardino, CA
04 January 2015